KENN BIVINS

39 LESSONS

BOOKS 1-4

KENN BIVINS

39 LESSONS

BOOKS 1-4

The 39 Lessons Series is a collection of affirmations and lessons intended to promote self-esteem, wisdom and excellent decision making for children.
This compilation contains the first four books of the best-selling series.

39 Lessons for Boys is nuggets of wisdom and sage advice for boys of all ages.

39 Lessons for Girls is nuggets of wisdom and sage advice for girls of all ages.

39 Lessons for Teens is nuggets of wisdom and sage advice for adolescent girls and boys. It addresses specific interests like sex, appearance, attitude and friendships.

39 Lessons for Black Boys & Girls is a series of affirmations and lessons that promote self-esteem, education, justice and wisdom among Black children of all ages.

I hope you enjoy reading and sharing this entire series with your precious ones. Thank you for reading.

love, laughter and power forever,
Kenn Bivins

39 LESSONS FOR BOYS

KENN BIVINS

KENN BIVINS

39 LESSONS FOR BOYS

for kenn and spencer

It is easier to build strong children than to repair broken men.
— Frederick Douglass

The legacy of a father is what he leaves in his stead for his children and those who have been in the shadow of his influence. I love my sons and the following are 39 lessons or snippets of wisdom I hope to teach (or have taught) them over the years.

If you have a son, nephew, mentee or boy in your life, you may benefit from this addendum to what you're already teaching. This is not a comprehensive list, but more so a foundation to build upon.

love and laughter forever,
Kenn Bivins

01

FOR BOYS

MANHOOD IS EARNED, NOT INHERITED

The biological emergence of becoming a man should not be confused with manhood. Manhood is accepting responsibility for yourself and your actions, tending to the care and well-being of others and contributing to society.

02

FOR BOYS

THERE IS A GOD...

Acknowledging that there is a being greater than yourself, creates a sense of purpose and humility that fuels endless curiosity, seeking and learning.

03

FOR BOYS

YOU ARE NOT HIM

Don't be judgemental. Instead, be humble and know that everyone makes mistakes while deserving the same grace you've been given.

04

FOR BOYS

BUT GOD DID MAKE YOU SPECIAL

The same God that made the universe made you intentionally. No one else is like you. That is your superpower.

05

FOR BOYS

GIVE MORE THAN YOU TAKE

Always give back to the faces and spaces that you took from.

06

FOR BOYS

DON'T RUN WITH THE CROWD, UNLESS YOU'RE THE LEADER

Lead, aspire to lead or,

while you're following,

learn to lead.

07

FOR BOYS

MAKE YOUR LIFE YOUR WORK

Find your purpose and make a living there.

08

FOR BOYS

NEVER MAKE WORK YOUR LIFE

Simply getting a paycheck is not,
and should never be all there is.

09

FOR BOYS

LOSING IS A SIGN THAT YOU'RE TRYING

~~~~

Losing is only temporary. Keep trying and learn from your losses.
You will win.

10

FOR BOYS

NEVER NEVER NEVER GIVE UP

Never.

11

FOR BOYS

NO ONE OWES YOU ANYTHING

Always be willing to work for what you want.

12

FOR BOYS

TRUE EDUCATION STARTS WHERE SCHOOL ENDS

Schooling is for the sake of demonstrating your aptitude to learn. Once you complete school, that ability is challenged and matured for the rest of your life. Therein true education ensues.

13

FOR BOYS

MONEY IS NOT EQUAL TO SUCCESS

Success is setting a goal and making it.

14

FOR BOYS

NEVER LOSE SELF-CONTROL (UNLESS YOU WANT TO)

It's called self-control because you are in control of self. Don't let anyone have mastery over you that leads you to lose self-control.

15

FOR BOYS

HEALTHY RELATIONSHIPS ARE BUILT ON COMMUNICATION WHICH LEADS TO TRUST

Talking and listening build a strong rapport.

16

FOR BOYS

PHYSICAL CONFRONTATION WITH A GIRL/WOMAN = LOSE/LOSE ODDS

There is no justification for violently putting your hands on a girl or a woman.

17

FOR BOYS

CREDIT CARD DEBT IS A BRUTAL MASTER

Use credit to build wealth.

18

FOR BOYS

IF YOU CAN'T AFFORD IT WITH CASH, SAVE FOR IT OR PASS IT BY

Disciplining yourself in this way will save you from the heartache of buyer's remorse and you'll value your purchases so much more when you take the time to consider them.

19

FOR BOYS

LEARNING STARTS WITH LEAVING YOUR COMFORT ZONE

If you don't challenge yourself, you won't grow.

20

FOR BOYS

INVEST IN TEACHING OTHERS WHAT YOU LEARN

And again, give back.

21

FOR BOYS

LOVE YOURSELF BEFORE YOU EXPECT A GIRL/WOMAN TO LOVE YOU

You inform others how to love you based on how you love yourself.

22

FOR BOYS

NEVER POINT A GUN THAT YOU'RE NOT PREPARED TO SHOOT

Literally and figuratively. Don't start something that you're not willing and ready to finish.

23

FOR BOYS

SOME FIGHTS ARE BEST WON BY WALKING AWAY

Every disagreement shouldn't be addressed with physical fighting. You can win many confrontations by walking away because the best victory is living to fight another day.

24

FOR BOYS

DON'T JUDGE OTHERS JUST BECAUSE THEY ARE DIFFERENT FROM YOU

You are not God.

25

FOR BOYS

LEARN FROM THE MISTAKES OF OTHERS

Julius Caesar was wrong. Experience is not the best teacher. There can be powerful lessons yielded from experience, but there also is great wisdom gleaned from the mistakes of others.

26

FOR BOYS

SAVE MORE THAN YOU SPEND

If you heed this lesson, you will be wealthy by the time you're 40.

27

FOR BOYS

GIRLS/WOMEN THINK COMPLETELY DIFFERENT FROM YOU

Learning of her and how she communicates is essential if you want to truly know her.

28

FOR BOYS

CELEBRATE THE DIFFERENCES

We were created to be different;
therefore we should celebrate that.

29

FOR BOYS

GIVE RESPECT TO OTHERS

How you treat others informs them how to treat you.

30

FOR BOYS

LET YOUR PRESENCE COMMAND RESPECT FROM ALL

– – – –

Hold your head high. You are the sun.

31

FOR BOYS

GIVE THANKS DAILY FOR WHAT YOU HAVE

~~~

A thankful heart is a humble and happy heart.

32

FOR BOYS

IT'S OKAY TO CRY

Crying is a byproduct of emotion that is a trait of being human. Don't be ashamed to feel all of your feelings.

33

FOR BOYS

SMILE MORE THAN YOU FROWN

It's easier to dwell on the negative things. Challenge yourself to smile even then. People treat you differently when you smile.

34

FOR BOYS

STAND UP STRAIGHT

Remember? You are the sun. And the sun only sets at dusk.

35

FOR BOYS

(ALMOST ALWAYS) TELL THE TRUTH

Practice living in your truth always. Know when your truth (your business) isn't for everyone to hear.

36

FOR BOYS

LOOK PEOPLE IN THE EYES
WHEN YOU TALK TO THEM

Some will need to indulge the fire in your eyes, while others will starve to see the humanity there.

37

FOR BOYS

ALWAYS GET THERE EARLY

When you're early, you're less stressed, you're ready for the unexpected, you get the best seat and you're always on time.

38

FOR BOYS

ALWAYS CONSIDER THE CONSEQUENCE

And take responsibility there.

39

FOR BOYS

SEEK GOD ALWAYS

Therein you'll find your purpose.

I am the dad I always wanted. My own father was absent, but I refused to let that color the type of parent I would be to my own sons.

I will admit that more than half the time, I had no clue what I was doing, but where I was green, God, grace and gummy bears covered me.
Yes, gummy bears. Boys love gummy bears.

While I was being Dad and teaching my sons, I was learning some things too. In the next few bonus pages, I want to share those things I lovingly call
4 Lessons for Big Boys.

BONUS 1

FOR BOYS

BE PRESENT

Any male can father a child, but it takes
a real man to **be** a father to his child.

Whether divorce, distance, finance or anything,
there is no excuse why a man shouldn't
be present for his child or children.

BONUS 2

FOR BOYS

BE KIND

"Man up" is not something you say to a boy.
He's not a man. He's a boy.

While you're teaching him resilience, do not discourage him with bitter words. Encourage him in kindness with equal measure of discipline.

BONUS 3

FOR BOYS

BE A FRIEND

~ ~ ~ ~ ~

Our children learn about relationships from us.
It's healthy for them to see us in friendships beyond
family members so that they know how to be a friend.

I think someone great once said,
"Be the friend you want to be."

BONUS 4

FOR BOYS

BE HUMBLE

No matter how awesome, blessed, handsome, intelligent or rich you are, be humble. Confidence is a great suit, but wear it with balance or life will remind you that you're not as _____ as you think.

It's better to be humble than to be humbled.

THE SIGNIFICANCE OF 39

You may be wondering, "What's the deal with 39? Why wasn't this book called 101 Lessons or something like that? 39 is just odd."

Well, let me explain. Years ago when I was blogging regularly, I went through what I lovingly regard as my "list phase." Lists are an amazing way to quantify accomplishments, goals, things to do, groceries, etc.

I ran across an internet challenge to detail random things about myself and this turned into a post titled "99 Things." This was my inaugural list, but it got so much feedback that I challenged myself further to write another list and then another, each one being a quantity divisible by 3 and ending in 9. Apparently, I was also into numeric themes.

Fun fact: June is my favorite month. It's a reflective time because so many events happen that month that are significant to me. Father's Day, being among those events, prompted me to write a list from a dad's perspective. My numbering pattern had landed on 39 around the time this list was conjured and thus was born **39 Lessons for Boys**.

Numerology indicates that 39 is associated with direction and guidance in discovering life's purpose. While I didn't know this at the time of the original writing, it's kismet how that worked out.

It's amazing to me how what seems so random can actually have meaning after all. So there you have it — the significance of 39.

love and laughter forever,
kenn

A STUDY GUIDE OF 21

What are lessons without study guides, right?
The following is a bonus list of lessons that I gleaned from the internet for the sake of open discussion and interpretation with your child.

These snippets can be savored by adults too, as reminders or principles to consider. Enjoy!

1. YOU ARE BEAUTIFUL.

2. LOVE YOURSELF.

3. TALK TO GOD DAILY.

4. ASK TOO MANY QUESTIONS.

5. IT'S OKAY TO NOT HAVE ALL THE ANSWERS.

6. SOME TIMES, BABY STEPS.

7. CHOOSE LIFE EVERYDAY.

8. LIFE DOESN'T COME IN FANCY WRAPPING, BUT IT'S STILL A GIFT.

9. DON'T DO ANYTHING YOU DON'T WANT TO DO.

10. DON'T APOLOGIZE FOR WHO YOU ARE.

11. FRAME DECISIONS WITH, "WILL THIS MATTER TOMORROW? IN FIVE YEARS?"

12. DO WHAT YOU SAY.

13. HOWEVER GOOD OR BAD THE SITUATION IS, IT WILL/ALWAYS/CHANGE.

14. DON'T RUSH IT. UNLESS YOU'RE RACING.

15. YOUR BODY ISN'T WHO YOU ARE. YOUR CHARACTER IS.

16. STOP OVERTHINKING.

17. CRYING WITH SOMEONE IS BETTER THAN HEALING ALONE.

18. NOTHING LASTS FOREVER.

19. BEFORE YOU DO GREAT THINGS, DO THE SMALL THINGS WELL.

20. GOD LOVES YOU BECAUSE OF WHO GOD IS, NOT BECAUSE OF ANYTHING THAT YOU'VE DONE OR DIDN'T DO.

21. STAY CURIOUS.

JOHN ROUSE

39
LESSONS
FOR GIRLS

KENN BIVINS

39 LESSONS FOR GIRLS

for nori

It is easier to build strong children than to repair broken ~~men~~ women.

— Frederick Douglass

paraphrased by Kenn Bivins

The legacy of a father is what he leaves in his stead for his children and those who have been in the shadow of his influence. I love my goddaughter and the following are 39 lessons or snippets of wisdom I hope to teach her as she matures into a young lady.

If you have a daughter, niece, mentee or girl in your life, you may benefit from this addendum to what you're already teaching. This is not a comprehensive list, but more so a foundation to build upon.

love and laughter forever,
Kenn Bivins

01

FOR GIRLS

YOU ARE GOOD ENOUGH

~ ~ ~

Your value is not implied by what any other person thinks or says of you.

02

FOR GIRLS

YOU DON'T HAVE TO BE A PRINCESS TO BE PRECIOUS

Many fables and fantasies have given girls the impression they have to be royalty to be considered special.

You're special whether you want to be a princess or not.

03

FOR GIRLS

STOP TRYING SO HARD TO FIT IN

You were made to stand out.

04

FOR GIRLS

THERE IS A GOD

Acknowledging that there is a being greater than yourself, creates a sense of purpose and humility that fuels endless curiosity, seeking and learning.

05

FOR GIRLS

YOU ARE NOT HIM (OR HER)

Be humble. You're awesome, but you're not God, so don't judge others. Instead, offer others the same grace you've been given because none of us are perfect.

06

FOR GIRLS

DON'T BE A MEAN GIRL

Be kind to others in the same way you want others to be kind to you. Give no regard to the actual mean girl. Don't let her energy define yours.

07

FOR GIRLS

A PRINCESS EVENTUALLY BECOMES A QUEEN

All things full of life will grow and become something greater today than yesterday.

08

FOR GIRLS

GOD INTENDED YOU

God intentionally made you.
You're as original as a snowflake or fingerprint.
Your glory is your difference.

Be you.

09

FOR GIRLS

YOUR BEST ACCESSORY IS YOUR SMILE

The mirror, the masses and I say so.

10

FOR GIRLS

BUT YOU DON'T HAVE TO SMILE IF YOU DON'T WANT TO

~ ~ ~ ~

While others benefit from seeing you smile, no one can make you do so. Your smile and the rest of your body belongs to you. Do with it what you choose.

11

FOR GIRLS

BE HEARD

Your voice, your presence and your influence matters.
Don't be afraid to speak up.

12

FOR GIRLS

BE QUIET

Listen to others. There will be times where you will gain much more knowledge by simply listening and observing.

13

FOR GIRLS

CAN'T NEVER COULD

Believe "I can" more than you fear "I can't."

14

FOR GIRLS

FAILURE IS NOT FINAL

A major ingredient of success is failing. Learn from your mistakes and missteps. Allow them to fuel you toward success.

15

FOR GIRLS

NEVER NEVER NEVER GIVE UP

Never.

16

FOR GIRLS

DON'T RUN WITH THE CROWD UNLESS YOU'RE THE LEADER

Lead, aspire to lead or, while you're following, learn to lead.

17

FOR GIRLS

YOU'RE NOT HER, BUT SHE'S NOT YOU

While you wish you were someone else, someone else is wishing she were you. Don't envy others.

18

FOR GIRLS

SAVE

Save your money, your words, your time and your body for the most deserving.

19

FOR GIRLS

PAY ATTENTION

Rather than listening to what people say, listen to what they do.

20

FOR GIRLS

LOVE YOURSELF

Set the standard for how you deserve to be loved by loving the girl in the mirror first.

21

FOR GIRLS

CREDIT CARD DEBT IS A BRUTAL MASTER

~ ~ ~ ~

Use credit to build wealth.

22

FOR GIRLS

HE CANNOT COMPLETE YOU

You are already whole. Anyone that is added to your life can only be an addendum to the awesome being that you already are.

23

FOR GIRLS

BE A BIG SISTER

Whether you have a sibling or not, seek others to nurture and teach. It will enhance your purpose or better inform you of it.

24

FOR GIRLS

FOLLOW YOUR HEART, BUT DON'T FORGET TO TAKE YOUR BRAIN WITH YOU

Give consideration to your feelings because you can't trust them all on their own.

25

FOR GIRLS

BOYS/MEN THINK COMPLETELY DIFFERENT THAN YOU

Learning of him and how he communicates is essential if you want to truly know him.

26

FOR GIRLS

GET OVER YOURSELF

Sometimes, it's not everyone else who is wrong. Sometimes it's you. Take a step back and take responsibility where it applies.

27

FOR GIRLS

GIVE THANKS

A thankful heart is a humble and happy heart.

28

FOR GIRLS

TRUE EDUCATION STARTS WHERE SCHOOL ENDS

Schooling is for the sake of demonstrating your aptitude to learn. Once you complete school, that ability is challenged and matured for the rest of your life. Therein true education ensues.

29

FOR GIRLS

YOU ARE ADDRESSED ACCORDING TO HOW YOU DRESS

Be mindful of this, especially concerning job interviews and boys.

30

FOR GIRLS

NOTHING LASTS FOREVER

A bad mood, heartbreak and acne will soon pass.

Be patient.

31

FOR GIRLS

DON'T WAGE WAR

Be careful of the things you say about and to people. Words can deeply hurt and are non-refundable.

32

FOR GIRLS

BUT BE A WARRIOR

You have an innate ability to overcome much.
You are stronger than you think.

33

FOR GIRLS

NOT EVERYONE WILL LIKE YOU AND THAT'S OKAY

There's nothing wrong with you just like there's nothing wrong with a sunny day, but some people don't like sunny days. They may prefer cloudy days because they're sensitive to sunlight.

You're like a sunny day ☀

34

FOR GIRLS

YOU ARE NOT YOUR PARENTS' MISTAKES

Your parents aren't perfect. Don't let their mistakes define your identity. Be your own person and grow in your own sense of self.

35

FOR GIRLS

DON'T SETTLE

Dust settles. You shouldn't. Ever.

36

FOR GIRLS

STAND TALL

Confidence attracts the best thoughts,
the right attitude and the coolest people.

37

FOR GIRLS

DON'T DOUBT YOURSELF

~~~~

You can do anything you set your mind to. Taking one step forward is all the persistence, belief and determination you will ever need.

38

FOR GIRLS

ALWAYS GET THERE EARLY

When you're early, you're less stressed, you're ready for the unexpected, you get the best seat and you're always on time.

39

FOR GIRLS

SEEK GOD ALWAYS

Therein you'll find your purpose.

I am the dad I always wanted. My own father was absent, but I refuse to let that color the type of influence I have with my goddaughter.

I'm honored that her mom trusts me enough to play such a significant role in her daughter's development. I must admit I have no clue what I'm doing at times, but where I'm a novice, God, grace and ice cream with sprinkles cover me. Yes, ice cream with sprinkles. Girls love ice cream with sprinkles.

While being a surrogate dad, I've pondered what type of woman I envision my goddaughter becoming, which has made me look at women differently. In the next few bonus pages, I want to share some observations I lovingly call "**4 Lessons for Big Girls.**"

BONUS 1

FOR GIRLS

BE A CONFIDANT

If you listen and engage her while she's sharing the small, unimportant things, she is more likely to trust sharing with you the more significant things when they happen.

BONUS 2

FOR GIRLS

BE CONSISTENT

She may not seem like she's paying attention to you, but she is. She internalizes what you do more than what you say.

BONUS 3

FOR GIRLS

BE A FRIEND

Nourish her creative side. It will help her see the world in new ways while encouraging free-thinking, problem-solving and producing.

BONUS 4

FOR GIRLS

BE HER

Put yourself in her shoes to understand her better. Encourage her where she is while nudging her toward who she might become.

KENN BIVINS

39 LESSONS FOR TEENS

for the 15-year old
version of me

and all teenagers thereafter

I am invisible, understand, simply because people refuse to see me.

— Ralph Ellison, *Invisible Man*

Being a teenager is hard. Hormones, homework, arrogance, inexplicable angst and outside influences are the bane of their existence and can tax your relationship with them. I've been on both sides of that coin, both as a teen and as a dad. I understand.

If you have a teenager in your life, you may benefit from this addendum to what you're already teaching. This is not a comprehensive list, but more so a foundation to build upon.

love and laughter forever,
Kenn Bivins

01

FOR TEENS

YOU MATTER

You, your voice and your presence matters.
The world has more hope with you in it.

02

FOR TEENS

DON'T COMPARE YOURSELF TO OTHERS

You'll never discover who you are if you measure your value by the stature of others. Honor who you were meant to be and spend your time celebrating your unique talents, voice, traits and purpose.

03

FOR TEENS

TAKE YOUR TIME

Childhood is a very short season.
Don't be in such a hurry to grow up.
You have the rest of your life to be an adult.

04

FOR TEENS

LOVE YOURS

Learn to love the life that you have,
love the person in the mirror and be thankful
for what you already have.

05

FOR TEENS

THIS IS TEMPORARY

Whatever painful or uncomfortable thing you're dealing with, know that it will eventually pass.

06

FOR TEENS

ACNE IS NOT FOREVER

One day, your skin will clear up, just as those problems that make you want to run away from your life.
It will get better.

07

FOR TEENS

THE INTERNET IS FOREVER

Nothing lasts forever, but the Internet does. Be careful of what you post and publicly share. Even though you may delete it, it will forever reside on a server or in a database for someone to someday access.

08

FOR TEENS

DO SOMETHING TODAY FOR THE FIRST TIME

Trying new things encourages a healthy mindset.

09

FOR TEENS

CELEBRATE YOURSELF

It doesn't have to be your birthday for you to honor who you are and your accomplishments, big and small.

10

FOR TEENS

DRINK MORE WATER

Odds are you're probably not drinking enough water to offset the sugary snacks and fried foods you love so much. Drink more water.

11

FOR TEENS

WASH YOUR FACE

Practicing good hygiene is not only good for your appearance, but it's also important that you present the best version of yourself. Be clean, be neat and don't stink :)

12

FOR TEENS

WASH YOUR SPACE

A clean body doesn't wear dirty clothes. By the same token, your environment informs what is in it. The appearance of your environment can affect your mindset.

13

FOR TEENS

YOUR BODY IS YOUR OWN

No one has authority over your body but you.

14

FOR TEENS

POVERTY IS OFTEN BORN OF UNPROTECTED PENISES

Becoming a parent prematurely and while you're still a child increases the likelihood of a difficult life - financially and otherwise. If you are having sex, use condoms.

15

FOR TEENS

WITH SEX COMES RESPONSIBILITY

The only safe sex is no sex. There is a great deal of responsibility that goes with physical intimacy, including the risk of pregnancy, unwanted diseases and emotional insecurity.

16

FOR TEENS

SEX IS NOT EQUAL TO LOVE

Love is about selfless, mutual respect and wanting what best for one another. Sex, outside of love, is simply for physical satisfaction that more often leads to low self-worth and diminishes self-respect.

17

FOR TEENS

SAVE SOME

Enjoy life, but don't spend all you have at once.
This is regarding money, time and yourself.

18

FOR TEENS

SAYING THANK YOU IS NOT THE SAME AS BEING THANKFUL

Say what you feel and feel what you say.

19

FOR TEENS

SARCASM IS NOT A LANGUAGE

Don't mistake a sense of humor with a form of communication. Sarcasm can be confusing, mocking and insulting to the listener who's not in on the joke. It also weakens communication skills.

20

FOR TEENS

RESPECT

Command respect from others just as you choose to give respect to them.

21

FOR TEENS

ADULTS ARE NOT PERFECT

They're human too, just a little bit older. Be patient with them. They're likely doing the best they know.

22

FOR TEENS

GET TO KNOW YOUR PARENTS

You can discover a lot about yourself by learning who your parents were when they were teenagers.

23

FOR TEENS

FIND A MENTOR

You will go further and with less frustration by going with someone who has walked the same path before. A mentor is someone who is trusted, mature-minded and a cheerleader all rolled into one. He or she can help you become a better version of yourself.

24

FOR TEENS

SHOW. DON'T TELL.

Let your verbs be your words.
Don't just talk about it. Be about it.

25

FOR TEENS

LET YOUR YES BE YES AND YOUR NO BE NO

Keep your word and fulfill your promises.
Don't offer a promise that you don't intend to keep.
Follow through.

26

FOR TEENS

HELP OUT

Don't wait for someone to ask for your help. If you see something that you can assist with, just do it. The feeling that results from helping others is invaluable.

27

FOR TEENS

LEARN HOW TO COUNT

Make a difference that is. Find your purpose and flourish there.

28

FOR TEENS

EVERYONE YOU WILL MEET WILL KNOW SOMETHING YOU DON'T

Approach others with a sense of wonder, respect and curiosity.

29

FOR TEENS

YOU DON'T KNOW IT ALL

No matter how smart you are, you will always have something to learn. Don't be arrogant with the knowledge and expertise that you do have.

30

FOR TEENS

IN FIVE YEARS, WHAT HAPPENS IN HIGH SCHOOL WON'T MATTER

What you're stressing about today won't matter so much tomorrow.

31

FOR TEENS

STUDY. PREPARE. PLAN.

Always. In school and in life.

32

FOR TEENS

A JOB IS FOR LOOSE CHANGE

Work hard, but be aware that there is more to life.

33

FOR TEENS

A CAREER IS FOR LIFE CHANGE

Invest in working hard at something that you love and therein, you might find both purpose and happiness.

34

FOR TEENS

SOMEONE DOES UNDERSTAND YOU

~ ~ ~

You're not the only one going through what you're going through.

You are not alone. You are not the only one.

35

FOR TEENS

DEPRESSION AND ANGER SHOULD BE EXPRESSED

Don't be ashamed of your feelings. You have the right to them. Write, draw, sing, play or do whatever constructive thing to cope. But above all, talk to someone. When we're sad or angry, we don't think clearly. Get help.

36

FOR TEENS

SING, DANCE AND PLAY AIR GUITAR

Have fun. Life is short. Make your own kind of music.

37

FOR TEENS

LISTEN

The world around you is saying so much.
Listen to what is said as well as what isn't.

38

FOR TEENS

WATCH

There is so much to see. Pay attention to the little things and the behaviors in the space you occupy.

39

FOR TEENS

SEEK GOD ALWAYS

Whether you know God or not, continually seek for answers.

You are the dream. Discover the dreamer.

I am the dad I always wanted. My own father was absent, but I refused to let that color the type of influence I would have on my sons and with my goddaughter.

The teenager phase of parenting can be tough. In the next few bonus pages, I want to share some observations that may give you, as a parent, strength that I lovingly call "**4 Lessons for Former Teens.**"

BONUS 1

FOR TEENS

BE PATIENT

You weren't always the most respectful.
You didn't always listen. Once upon a time, you may
have even been self-centered.

But then you grew up.
It will happen with your teen, as well.

BONUS 2

FOR TEENS

BE THERE

They may act as if they don't care about what you have to say or your presence, but they do.
Be physically and emotionally present because they will indeed need you to be.

BONUS 3

FOR TEENS

BE SMARTER

Your child navigates in spaces that you need to be knowledgeable of. The whole world has access to them through digital technology. Don't be afraid of it.

BONUS 4

FOR TEENS

BE PATIENT

And I'll repeat it because hormones, arrogance, inexplicable angst and outside influences will tax your relationship with your child.

This is a phase. They will eventually grow past it. Be patient.

KENN BIVINS

39 LESSONS FOR BLACK BOYS & GIRLS

for boys and girls
of all shades of Black.

Being Black isn't a trend or a sin.
It's the skin and the lessons within.

— Kenn Bivins

First of all, why is this book necessary? Isn't the title somewhat divisive? What does this book have to say that the previous ones in the 39 Lessons series didn't already say? This book is about race – specifically the Black race.

Being Black in the United States, or anywhere else for that matter, is a nuanced experience. It is within those layers, if left unaddressed, that identity can be lost.
So we must talk to our Black children about race.

If it's treated as a taboo topic, imagine how powerless and unloved Black children may eventually feel. Oh, and while this book is addressed to them, it's for children of every race to enjoy.

love and power forever,
Kenn Bivins

01

FOR BLACK BOYS & GIRLS

YOUR BLACK IS BEAUTIFUL.

Your melanin, strength, creativity, versatility, faith, tenacity and intuition make you inherently beautiful.

02

FOR BLACK BOYS & GIRLS

YOUR SKIN DOES NOT MAKE YOU...

a suspect, villain, thug, n-word, b-word, criminal, brute, freak, or any negative thing. Your skin is instead the wrapper to all of the good things within.

03

FOR BLACK BOYS & GIRLS

YOU CAN'T BE A KING AND A N-WORD.

- - - -

The bloodied, oppressive *n-word* can't be saved and ushered into camaraderie. Abandon using it to refer to your people. Instead, think and speak greater destinies about yourself and your loved ones.

04

FOR BLACK BOYS & GIRLS

YOU CAN'T BE A QUEEN AND A B-WORD.

A *b-word* is a female dog, or a person or thing that is very difficult. It is usually leveraged as an insult against a woman or a person perceived to be weak and inferior. You are greater than those things. Hold your head higher that they might see your crown.

05

FOR BLACK BOYS & GIRLS

THERE IS SO MUCH MORE TO YOUR HISTORY THAN SLAVERY.

We have contributed to innovations, science, literature, art and customs that have helped shape the culture of the United States and the world. Despite slavery, we found ways to survive and thrive beyond.

06

FOR BLACK BOYS & GIRLS

MINDSET IS YOUR SUPERPOWER.

Persistence, hard work and effort are all very important traits to have, but having that foundational belief that you are in control of your own destiny is the secret sauce to your success.

07

FOR BLACK BOYS & GIRLS

YOU ARE NOT A MINORITY.

Black people's cultural influence on the mainstream alongside their economic power and innovation has long established them as the foundation to mankind. And logically, people who are of the global majority can't be considered minorities.

08

FOR BLACK BOYS & GIRLS

THE WAY THEY SEE YOU SHOULD NEVER TAINT THE WAY YOU SEE YOURSELF.

You can't control what others think about you, but you can command what you think of yourself.

09

FOR BLACK BOYS & GIRLS

YOUR LIFE MATTERS.

- - - -

Ignore the subtle diminishing of your value in the media, in the justice system, in education and in white-washed history. You are good enough.

10

FOR BLACK BOYS & GIRLS

READ A BOOK.
READ MANY BOOKS.

~ ~ ~ ~

Reading books increases knowledge, reduces stress, expands vocabulary, builds analytical skills, improves memory, focus and writing skills, and is a great form of entertainment.

11

FOR BLACK BOYS & GIRLS

STUDY. PRACTICE. REPEAT.

There is no glory in practice,
but without practice there is no glory.

12

FOR BLACK BOYS & GIRLS

COLUMBUS DAY, THANKSGIVING, EMANCIPATION PROCLAMATION, ETC.

White-wash: to alter something in a way that favors, features or caters to White people, such as increasing their prominence, relevance or impact while minimizing or misrepresenting that of non-White people.

13

FOR BLACK BOYS & GIRLS

JUNETEENTH IS...

the June 19th celebration of the real liberation from slavery that came two and a half years after the Emancipation Proclamation was issued on January 1, 1863. 250,000 slaves in Texas were already free — but none of them knew it and no one was in a hurry to tell them.

14

FOR BLACK BOYS & GIRLS

MARCUS GARVEY, PRIDE AND INNOVATION

He was a writer, gifted speaker and activist who established a corporation that offered stock for Black people to buy. The project generated income and provided jobs. There were numerous enterprises, including a chain of grocery stores and restaurants, a steam laundry, tailor shops, a publishing house and a doll factory.

15

FOR BLACK BOYS & GIRLS

IDA B. WELLS,
COURAGE AND EMPATHY

She was an unsung American hero, a journalist and an activist who investigated and reported lynchings all the way to the White House, calling for reforms. She was described as a woman with plenty of nerve who was as smart as a steel trap. She also fought for Black women's rights long before it was popular or safe.

16

FOR BLACK BOYS & GIRLS

KATHERINE JOHNSON, GENIUS AND PERSEVERANCE

She was the mathematician who hand-calculated the trajectory for America's first trip to space. Despite segregation and discrimination, her calculations would be critical to the success of NASA's crewed space flights.

17

ELLEN AND WILLIAM CRAFT, CUNNING AND RESOURCEFUL

The Crafts were a married couple who wanted to start a family so they escaped slavery by hiding in plain sight. Ellen resembled a White woman, so she cross-dressed as a male plantation owner, with William posing as her slave. They fled Georgia and lived in England for 19 years before returning to the United States and establishing a farm.

18

FOR BLACK BOYS & GIRLS

RACISM IS ALIVE AND WELL IN AMERICA.

When Barack Obama was elected the first Black president, racism didn't suddenly die. It simply evolved to thrive publicly in the form of legislation and policies that meshed bigoted ideologies with white-washed ignorance.

19

FOR BLACK BOYS & GIRLS

YOU DON'T HAVE THE SAME PRIVILEGE AS YOUR WHITE FRIENDS.

They're much less likely to be profiled by police, followed in a store, held accountable for others in their community, marginalized or judged according to the color of their skin. Be vigilant.

20

FOR BLACK BOYS & GIRLS

THEY ARE NOT BETTER THAN YOU.
YOU ARE NOT BETTER THAN THEM.

Don't be an entitled human or support entitled humans.

21

FOR BLACK BOYS & GIRLS

YOU BELONG TO THE AFRICAN DIASPORA.

Diaspora means the dispersion of people from their homeland or community. As a Black person, you are a part of the African diaspora because your ancestors were dispersed from the continent of Africa to parts all over the world because of the slave trade and colonization.

22

FOR BLACK BOYS & GIRLS

ALL LAWS ARE NOT JUST.

People who enact laws are empowered by widespread voter ignorance and by strong biases of their own. It was said by one of the founding fathers of the United States that if a law is unjust, a man is not only right to disobey it, he is obligated to do so.

23

FOR BLACK BOYS & GIRLS

PROTEST IS THE RIGHT TO SPEAK AGAINST WHAT IS WRONG.

Don't let anyone shame you out of standing for what you believe is right. The United States was founded on protest.

24

FOR BLACK BOYS & GIRLS

EQUALITY AND EQUITY ARE NOT THE SAME.

You will win $500 if you can fly your paper plane farther than your classmates.
Equality supplies all of you with sheets of paper although some of them are crumpled up.
Equity makes sure that all of you have the same quality of paper to start with.

25

FOR BLACK BOYS & GIRLS

THEIR ICE WATER IS NOT COLDER THAN YOURS.

Corporations, restaurants and institutions don't sell a better product simply because they're White-owned. This belief is rooted in self-hate. Support Black business.

26

FOR BLACK BOYS & GIRLS

MAKE YOUR VOICE HEARD.

Be confident, ask questions, challenge authority and interact as an equal.

27

FOR BLACK BOYS & GIRLS

A RIOT IS THE LANGUAGE OF THE UNHEARD.

And what is it America has failed to hear? It has failed to hear that the promises of freedom and justice have not been met. And it has failed to hear that large segments of White society are more concerned about tranquility and the status quo than about justice and humanity.
— Martin Luther King Jr.

28

FOR BLACK BOYS & GIRLS

WE ARE NOT MONOLITHIC.

To be monolithic is to act and think the same.
We are not limited because of our "color."
We are individuals who are different
from one another in thought, beliefs,
practices and other characteristics.

29

FOR BLACK BOYS & GIRLS

CULTURAL APPROPRIATION IS...

the act of adopting (stealing) elements of another culture, including knowledge, practices and symbols, without understanding or respecting the original culture and context.

30

FOR BLACK BOYS & GIRLS

MICROAGGRESSION IS...

brief and commonplace daily verbal, behavioral or environmental indignities, whether intentional or unintentional, that communicate hostile, derogatory or negative racial slights and insults toward people of color.

31

FOR BLACK BOYS & GIRLS

LOOK THEM IN THE EYE.

It demonstrates confidence and trustworthiness, while acknowledging the value of the other person.

32

FOR BLACK BOYS & GIRLS

EXPLORE BEYOND YOUR DOOR.

Whether it's leaving your neighborhood, your city, your state or your country, aspire to travel.

33

FOR BLACK BOYS & GIRLS

MASTER THE ART OF CODE-SWITCHING.

Code-switching is the ability to modify one's language, dialects, styles, registers and behavior to adapt to different cultural environments. It is an extremely valuable skill in almost any career.

34

FOR BLACK BOYS & GIRLS

TRUST YOUR GUT.

Guts. You've had them since you were born. Trust them.

35

FOR BLACK BOYS & GIRLS

DON'T MARGINALIZE YOURSELF WITH LABELS.

And don't allow others to do it, either. It's a form of control that can limit your full potential.

36

FOR BLACK BOYS & GIRLS

BE CONSCIOUS, AWAKE AND AWARE.

Be vigilant of racism in society and other forms of oppression and injustice.

37

FOR BLACK BOYS & GIRLS

TAKE.

Take advice, seek assistance, be curious and graciously receive praise.

38

FOR BLACK BOYS & GIRLS

GIVE.

Give back, provide assistance, offer resources and grant acclaim.

39

FOR BLACK BOYS & GIRLS

SEEK GOD ALWAYS.

Whether you know God or not, continually seek answers. You are the dream. Discover the dreamer.

With the other books in the 39 Lessons series, I coined the phrase "love and laughter forever," but you've probably noticed that's not the case with this one.

On the following pages I explain why "love and power forever" was more important to emphasize in this book.

LOVE

It is important to be loved and reminded of love by constant affirmations and actions. Unfortunately, the world our Black children go into every day conspires to tell them they are unlovable.

All children (that means you) are worthy of love, respect and consideration. Whether the world acknowledges it or not, our Black children must still love themselves. Love is a verb.

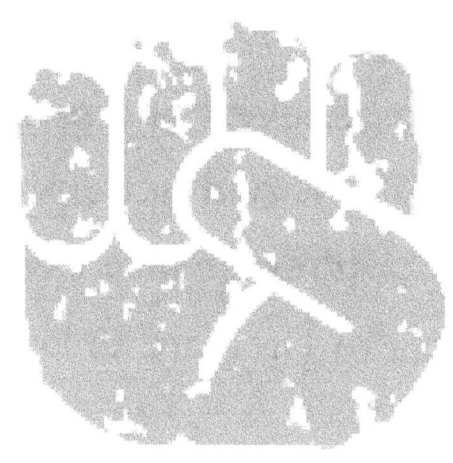

POWER

Laughter should be synonymous with childhood, but that's not a reality for many Black children. Some of them are in conditions and environments where they feel powerless, unheard and invisible.

When I was a child, I fantasized about having superpowers so I could defeat the odds against me and rescue others in need. Time revealed that I didn't need superpowers to be empowered. I had my presence, my resilience, my voice and a sense of self-esteem. A raised fist became like Superman's cape.

FOREVER

The ankh was used in Egyptian hieroglyphics and art to represent the word for "life" or the "key of life."

The ankh is more appropriate than the previously utilized star, considering the subject matter and the audience. Love and power should be asserted and internalized without ceasing. Forever.

ADVICE FOR THE PARENTS OF BLACK BOYS & GIRLS

Parents, let's admit it: The rules are different for our Black babies. This system hasn't failed them. This system wasn't built for them. It can be quite daunting to bring them up in an environment that is prone to hostility toward them, but all is not lost.

You can raise Black boys who are elated and full of joy, and Black girls who are confident and love themselves. While it is revolutionary to be Black, happy and unbothered in this country, it is possible.

The following tips are guides toward that progressive end.

1. TALK TO THEM ABOUT THE POLICE.
Manage a healthy and safe perspective of the police.

2. ASK, THEN LISTEN.
Ask them open-ended questions, as if you are the one learning. Listen intently to their answers.

3. ANSWER QUESTIONS.
Feed their curiosity about all things trivial and difficult, all the while building their trust.

4. TAKE A BREAK.
Don't teach them that life is solely about work. Teach them the concept of self-care along the way.

5. HAVE FAITH.
Demonstrate an active belief and faith in God.

6. EAT GOOD.
Serve and eat food that is healthy for mind and body.

7. SHARE YOUR STORY.
Tell who you were as a child so they can learn more about where and who they come from.

8. SHOW THEM THE MONEY.
Teach them about saving and investing.

9. PLAY OUTSIDE.
Spend time playing with them in the fresh air and sunshine.

10. TAKE THEM ON VACATION.
Get away together to relax and recharge.

11. READ TOGETHER.
Connect through books (like this one).

WHO IS KENN BIVINS?

Kenn Bivins is an illustrator turned author who has an affinity toward telling both heart-warming and heart-wrenching tales of redemption. Through his novels and non-fiction, he aspires for his readers to identify with the characters and themes that he crafts through suspense, intrigue, action and the unexpected.

His love of literature was conceived from the pages of comic books and honed by enjoying the literary works of Richard Wright, Ralph Ellison and John Steinbeck, among many.

His love for nurturing and encouraging children was born of him being a dad, a godfather, an uncle and a mentor.

His novels, **the Wedding & Disaster of Felona Mabel** and **Pious** have received much critical acclaim from the literary world.

A WORD FROM KENN

Thank you for taking the time to read and consider this very important collection. It's meant to be read multiple times and shared with loved ones. And by share, I mean tell people where and how to get their own copy or gift them one. Just between you and me, I've learned not to loan books because I never get them back ;)

Thank you again for being the awesome nurturer, superhero and loving human you were meant to be.

love, laughter and power forever,
Kenn Bivins

Copyright © 2020 by Kenn Bivins. All rights reserved.

No part of this publication may be used or reproduced in any manner whatsoever without written permission except in the case of brief quotations embodied in critical articles or reviews.

Published by Invisible Ennk Press.

All inquiries and correspondence received at:
Invisible Ennk Press
P.O. Box 69
Avondale Estates, GA 30002.

Library of Congress Cataloging-in-Publication Data is available.
LLCN 2020913785

ebook   ISBN: 978-1-7333747-9-8
paperback ISBN: 978-1-7354073-0-2
hardback   ISBN: 978-1-7354073-8-8

Design by Kenn Bivins.

www.ingramcontent.com/pod-product-compliance
Lightning Source LLC
Chambersburg PA
CBHW081238080526
44587CB00022B/3992